The Battle of Bunker Hill

by Mary Englar

Content Adviser: Brett Barker, Ph.D.,
Assistant Professor of History,
University of Wisconsin–Marathon County

Reading Adviser: Rosemary G. Palmer, Ph.D.,
Department of Literacy, College of Education,
Boise State University

Compass Point Books ✦ Minneapolis, Minnesota

Compass Point Books
3109 West 50th Street, #115
Minneapolis, MN 55410

Visit Compass Point Books on the Internet at *www.compasspointbooks.com*
or e-mail your request to *custserv@compasspointbooks.com*

On the cover: Detail from *The Death of General Warren at the Battle of Bunker Hill* by John Trumbull

Photographs ©: The Granger Collection, New York, cover, 5, 28, 33, 38; Prints Old & Rare, back cover (far left); Library of Congress, back cover, 31; North Wind Picture Archives, 6, 9, 10, 11, 15, 16, 19, 22, 24, 26, 29, 35, 41; Stock Montage, 12, 23; Yale Center for British Art, Paul Mellon Collection/The Bridgeman Art Library, 13; Massachusetts Historical Society, Boston, Massachusetts/The Bridgeman Art Library, 20; Time Life Pictures/Mansell/Getty Images, 30; Courtesy of Army Art Collection, U.S. Army Center of Military History, 32; Hulton Archive/Getty Images, 36; Stock Montage/Getty Images, 39; Private Collection/The Bridgeman Art Library, 40.

Editor: Sue Vander Hook
Page Production: Blue Tricycle, Bobbie Nuytten
Photo Researcher: Svetlana Zhurkin
Cartographer: XNR Productions, Inc.
Library Consultant: Kathleen Baxter

Creative Director: Keith Griffin
Editorial Director: Carol Jones
Managing Editor: Catherine Neitge

Library of Congress Cataloging-in-Publication Data
Englar, Mary.
    The Battle of Bunker Hill / by Mary Englar.
       p. cm. — (We the people)
    Includes bibliographical references and index.
    Audience: Grades 4-6.
    ISBN-13: 978-0-7565-2461-6 (library binding)
    ISBN-10: 0-7565-2461-X (library binding)
    1. Bunker Hill, Battle of, Boston, Mass., 1775—Juvenile literature.
    I. Title.
    E241.B9E63 2007
    973.3'312—dc22   2006027086

TABLE OF CONTENTS

A BLOODY BATTLE

The sun rose over foggy Boston Harbor in Massachusetts on the morning of June 17, 1775. In the dark hours before sunrise, Colonel William Prescott and more than 1,200 American colonists had dug trenches, strengthened fences, and built a dirt wall on top of Breed's Hill. Now Prescott watched as British warships anchored in the nearby Charles River. The sunlight would now expose the Americans to British troops.

Sailors aboard the British ship *Lively* spotted the colonists working on Breed's Hill and fired their cannons. Although most cannonballs fell short of their targets, the noise and smoke terrified Prescott's men. Most of these American soldiers were farmers who had never fought a battle.

Colonel Prescott jumped onto the makeshift wall and shouted encouragement to his men. Then he ordered them to finish their redoubt, or temporary defense structure,

Colonial militiamen built a mud wall on Breed's Hill to protect them from the British army.

5

Colonel William Prescott watched from Breed's Hill as British warships entered Boston Harbor.

before the British attacked. The sweaty, dirt-covered colonists returned to the wall. They were exhausted and hungry. Then a cannonball destroyed their water barrels.

Prescott and his men watched as British General William Howe and 1,200 of his soldiers rowed across the Charles River from Boston. When the British stepped onto Charlestown Peninsula, which led to Breed's Hill, the American colonists had finished their tasks and were prepared to fight to the death for their rights.

The colonists wanted a voice in new laws and taxes that affected them. They were angry with the British army for the recent American deaths at the battles at Lexington and Concord. With old muskets, little ammunition, and fewer men overall than the British, the Americans began the bloody battle on Breed's Hill. Oddly, it would come to be called the Battle of Bunker Hill, after another hill nearby.

7

No Taxation Without Representation

For more than 10 years before the Battle of Bunker Hill, American colonists had been protesting British tax laws. The first was the American Revenue Act in 1764. The Stamp Act of 1765 and the Townshend Duties of 1767 were even more unpopular. The new taxes meant colonists had to pay an additional cost for sugar, books, newspapers, legal documents, glass, paper, and tea.

Many colonists claimed Great Britain didn't have the right to tax them. They believed British subjects could be taxed only when their representatives in Parliament voted for new taxes. Because the colonists couldn't elect representatives to Parliament, they didn't think Parliament had the right to tax them.

British leaders claimed Parliament represented all British subjects, including American colonists. The colonists protested, however, and refused to pay the taxes. Their rallying cry became "No taxation without representation!" British tax collectors needed help, so they asked for British troops.

In 1768, Great Britain sent 1,800 soldiers to Boston to enforce the tax laws. The Boston colonists were forced to feed and house these soldiers. Dressed in their fine red uniforms, British troops often bullied colonists in the streets. The colonists were angry that they had lost some of their freedom.

Protesters burned stamped papers to show their disapproval of the Stamp Act.

The colonists' anger against the "Redcoats," as they mockingly called them, resulted in fistfights and beatings. In March 1770, a

9

British troops entered Boston to enforce taxation and other colonial laws.

conflict between British troops and Boston workers ended
in the death of five colonists. For more than a day, hundreds
of colonists roamed the streets of Boston. They wanted
revenge on the Redcoats for these killings that came to be
called the Boston Massacre.

10

The colonists organized boycotts of English products. Instead of buying British cloth, colonial women spun their own cloth. Colonists drank coffee to avoid buying English tea. The conflict over taxes grew. In late 1773, a group of colonists secretly boarded three British ships in Boston Harbor. They broke open hundreds of crates of tea and

Colonists threw crates of tea into Boston Harbor to protest British taxes.

11

dumped them into the ocean. This Boston Tea Party, as it came to be called, made the British very angry.

In 1774, England's Parliament passed the Coercive Acts to punish the people of Massachusetts Colony for destroying British merchandise. One of the acts closed the port of Boston to all trade. Nearly everyone in Boston worked in the shipping trade, so closing the port took away their jobs. It also stopped goods from coming into the city. Now colonists had to get by on what they could make themselves.

Another law took away the colonists'

The British Parliament met in London to make laws for Great Britain and its colonies.

12

right to govern them-selves. England's King George III appointed British General Thomas Gage to be governor of Massachusetts and commander of all British troops in the colonies.

Thousands of British soldiers were sent to Boston to enforce the new laws. King George declared that the port

British General Thomas Gage (1721–1787)

would stay closed until the colonists paid British merchants for the tea they had destroyed.

FALLEN PATRIOTS

The colonists sent letters to King George asking for a peaceful solution to their differences. They agreed they were subjects of Great Britain but repeated that they wanted a voice in new laws and taxes. The king, however, didn't agree.

By 1775, the colonists had reached a breaking point. They formed patriot militias, or citizen armies, to stand up to British troops. Every man between the ages of 16 and 60 served in this untrained army. Some of them were called Minutemen, who promised to show up to fight at a moment's notice. General Gage wrote to Parliament asking for more troops to end the protests by force.

In April, colonial spies learned that the British planned to arrest two American leaders, John Hancock and Samuel Adams, for organizing the Boston Tea Party. As word spread throughout Boston, Paul Revere and William Dawes left for Lexington, Massachusetts, on horseback

14

Paul Revere roused citizens along the road to Lexington to tell them that the British were coming.

to warn the colonists that the British were coming for
Hancock and Adams.

Meanwhile, at Lexington Green, an open grassy area
in the middle of Lexington, 50 American militiamen waited
for British troops to arrive. British Major John Pitcairn

Colonists battled the powerful British army on Lexington Green on April 19, 1775.

and his soldiers arrived first, ordering the patriots to put down their guns and leave. The Americans turned to go, but they didn't lay down their guns. Shots were fired. Eight Americans were killed and 10 wounded.

Word spread quickly that the British had shot colonists at Lexington. Minutemen grabbed their muskets and went to fight the British. But the colonists were outnumbered and retreated after a brief fight.

The Redcoats marched on to Concord. There, other colonial militias stood their ground, and the British turned and retreated toward Boston. All along the way, Minutemen, farmers, and townspeople fired at the Redcoats from behind fences and houses. The colonists killed or wounded 273 British soldiers that day and forced the rest back to Boston. The Americans lost 95 men.

The battle marked a turning point for the colonists. They realized the British were willing to kill them to prove that Great Britain ruled the colonies. But they also realized that they could fight back—and win.

17

BUILDING THE COLONIAL ARMY

After the victory at Lexington, thousands of colonists came to Boston to join the militia. These new soldiers surrounded Boston, set up their defenses, and blocked roads that led to the city. Ships were not allowed to enter the harbor, which meant goods could not be delivered. Soon the British army as well as the citizens of Boston didn't have enough fresh food.

General Artemas Ward and John Thomas, leaders of the Massachusetts militia, set up military headquarters at Cambridge, about 5 miles (8 kilometers) west of Boston. Volunteers arrived, ready to fight with whatever guns and ammunition they owned or borrowed, but few brought enough food or clothes. Local farmers supplied the militia with food, but more guns, ammunition, tents, and clothing were needed.

Ward asked the Massachusetts Provincial Congress, the colony's governing body, for help. If the Congress didn't

Colonial gunsmiths worked hard to make more guns for the Minutemen.

equip the army, Ward feared that the volunteers would
return to their homes. After all, most of the volunteers were
farmers, and spring planting needed to be done. It wouldn't
take much for them to go back to their farms. Ward was
right. As quickly as the volunteers arrived, some began

heading back home when they learned there were not enough supplies. Dr. Joseph Warren, a colonial leader, believed in the patriot cause and helped General Ward organize the militias. By late May 1775, however, Great Britain had sent 1,000 more troops and three generals to help General Gage.

Dr. Joseph Warren (1741–1775)

Knowing the colonists were preparing to fight, Gage called his generals to a council of war. They decided to take control of the highest hills around Boston.

To the south, they planned to take Dorchester

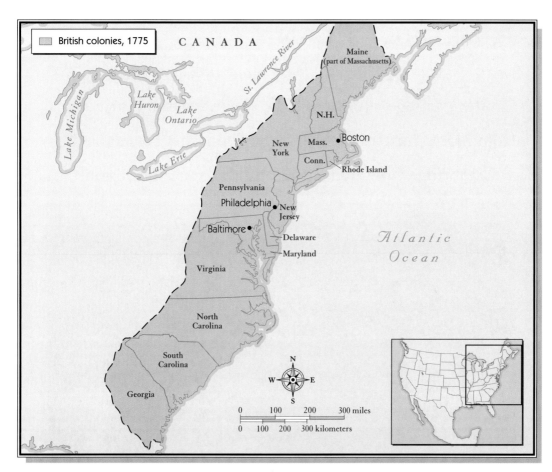

The Battle of Bunker Hill was fought in Massachusetts, one of the 13 original colonies.

Heights. To the north, they would take two hills—Bunker
Hill and Breed's Hill. But American spies learned about the
British plan and informed the American militias.

A Secret Plan

On the evening of June 16, 1775, about 800 militiamen from Massachusetts and 200 from Connecticut assembled at Cambridge Common, an area in the center of Boston.

Samuel Langdon, president of Harvard College, prayed for the colonial militiamen on Cambridge Common the night before the Battle of Bunker Hill.

Drums beat as men and boys of all ages fell into ranks. Each of them brought one day's provisions, a blanket, and digging tools. None wore uniforms, and most carried old muskets.

Colonel William Prescott was chosen to lead the Massachusetts men. The Connecticut group was led by General Israel Putnam.

The men moved quietly through the countryside of the peninsula on which Boston was located. A very

American General Israel Putnam (1718–1790)

small strip of land called the Charlestown Neck connected the peninsula to the mainland. At its widest, the strip was only 300 feet (91 meters).

The officers stopped to discuss their plans. Historians don't know what they discussed, but after the conference, Prescott led his men over Bunker Hill and set up camp on nearby Breed's Hill. At the highest point, Breed's Hill was 75 feet (23 m) and in range of British cannons in Boston. Bunker Hill, at 110 feet (34 m) high, was farther from the cannons.

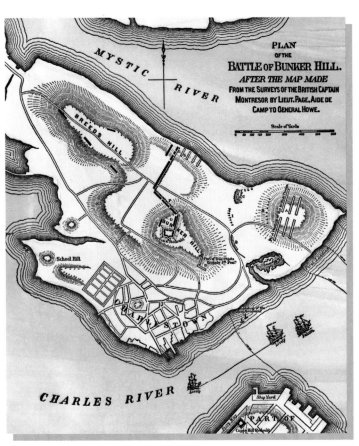

A map of the battle plan was drawn from a British map.

No one knows why the officers chose the lower hill, but it was not the better choice.

The men set up camp at midnight. Prescott ordered his engineer to stake out boundaries for a redoubt. In this case, it was a mud wall that would protect the troops during an attack. The walls would be about 160 feet (49 m) long on each side. A small door was built on the corner that faced Charlestown Neck, their only escape route to the mainland.

The men dug down several feet and used the dirt to make mud and build walls. They worked tirelessly throughout the night. Prescott sent 60 men along Charlestown Neck to the mainland to watch for any sign that the enemy had heard or seen them.

At the light of dawn, Prescott realized he had made a major mistake. To the left and right, they were completely open to British attack. If the British came on their right or up the Mystic River on the left, they could circle around behind them and cut off any escape. Prescott ordered some of his men to extend the wall on the left side. But he didn't

Colonists positioned their weapons and worked on their redoubt the night before battle.

have enough men to build a protection on the right flank.

At 4 A.M., British soldiers onboard the *Lively* in Boston Harbor began to fire at the peninsula. The explosives boomed across the water, and Bostonians jumped out of bed in fear. On the mainland, General Ward heard the cannons and knew the Americans had been discovered.

THE BATTLE BEGINS

As American militia braced themselves for an attack, General Gage ordered the other British generals to his home in Boston. They discussed plans of attack, but they couldn't agree.

General Clinton wanted to attack immediately from both the Charles River and the Mystic River flanks. He believed that would prevent any new troops from arriving and trap Prescott's men behind their wall. Gage and two other generals believed a direct attack from the front would easily finish off the colonists. They believed the colonists would turn and run when they came face-to-face with 2,000 well-trained British soldiers.

It took hours for the British generals to agree on a plan and for their troops to get organized. British General William Howe ordered his soldiers to pack fresh bread and meat, clean their guns, and dress in full uniform.

While the British prepared for battle, the Americans

27

worked frantically to finish more walls. Warren and other colonists arrived to help, which encouraged the tired men who had been working all night. But the Americans needed more men. Prescott sent for more colonists, and General Ward ordered the New Hampshire militia led by Colonel John Stark to come to Breed's Hill.

When Stark and his men arrived, they saw the weak flank on the side by the Mystic River and ran down the hill

New Hampshire militiamen traveled to Boston to take part in the Battle of Bunker Hill.

to build a stone wall on the beach. British warships on the Charles River started pounding the fort with cannon fire. They also fired their guns across the narrow piece of land at Charlestown Neck to prevent more Americans from crossing to the battleground.

Around 1 P.M., the British stepped on shore and began their march on land. More than 2,000 trained, well-equipped troops headed out to fight the colonists. General Howe sent some of his men to the beach of the Mystic River. The rest he ordered to line up. He would take half the men and attack the colonists on the Mystic River

British General William Howe (1729–1814)

29

flank. British General Robert Pigot would take the other half to attack the fort from the other side. Howe ordered his soldiers in Boston to fire red-hot cannon balls, which set fires wherever they landed. Soon Charlestown, the city next to Boston, was in flames.

Then Howe ordered the rest of his soldiers to advance up Breed's Hill. Six hundred British soldiers moved up the

British cannons battered the nearby city of Charlestown.

The powerful British army far outnumbered the colonial militia.

hill. Their heavy wool uniforms weighed them down. The heat, tall grass, and fences slowed their progress.

Above them, at the top of the hill, the Americans waited nervously. Since they had little ammunition, their officers told them to hold their fire until the British were so close they could see the whites of their eyes. Then they should aim their guns first at British officers.

The British along the Mystic River moved quickly along the flat beach. When they got close, Stark's men fired. The British were stopped in their tracks, and nearly 100 Redcoats lay dead on the shore. The front ranks fell, and the ranks behind them closed in. But Stark's men fired again, and the British turned and retreated down the beach.

Then the Americans opened fire on Howe's men marching up the hill. The blast of gunfire from the Americans didn't hit Howe, but his men fell dead all around him. The Americans fired again and hit more soldiers before the British could reload their muskets. Howe called a retreat, and the British ran down the hill to regroup.

At the clash atop Breed's Hill, more British died than colonists.

32

THE FINAL BATTLE

After British troops reorganized, Howe ordered a second attack. Marching up Breed's Hill where the bodies of their dead and wounded lay, British soldiers again tried to storm the wall. But the Americans pushed them back with deadly musket fire.

People in Boston watched the battle from rooftops as the orange flicker of muskets mowed down the British. Once again, Howe's men retreated.

The Americans celebrated their victory,

Many Bostonians who watched the battle had relatives and friends fighting on Breed's Hill.

33

but Colonel Prescott was worried. Many of his men had left the front lines because they were wounded or afraid. Prescott had only about 150 men left. These men had used nearly all their ammunition, and only a few officers had swords. If the British came over their walls, his men would be forced to fight with their bare hands.

Howe wanted to send his British soldiers up the hill to attack again, but he had lost too many men. He sent a messenger to Boston to ask General Clinton for reinforcements. Four hundred fresh soldiers arrived. This time, Howe ordered the men to take off their knapsacks and any extra gear, and carry only the supplies and weapons they needed. The men fell into columns and began their march up Breed's Hill.

When the British were close to the wall, the Americans fired. For a moment, Prescott believed the British would give up. But the British soldiers were angry and determined. They pushed on through the heavy fire. When the colonists ran out of ammunition, they began

British troops marched in strict formation up Breed's Hill.

firing anything they could find—nails or scraps of metal.
Some threw rocks.

The British rushed over the walls and used their bayonets to stab anyone in sight. It was dark and smoky from
the gunfire, and no one could tell who the enemy was.

35

Dr. Joseph Warren, popular American leader, was fatally wounded in the battle.

In the chaos of the battle, Joseph Warren was shot and killed. Prescott ordered his men to retreat, and many fled along narrow Charlestown Neck.

Colonel Stark's men ran to nearby Bunker Hill as they fired at the British. Stark's troops hid behind walls and trees and shot fiercely, but the British pursued them to the top of Bunker Hill. When Clinton saw the Americans retreating, he ordered soldiers to hold Bunker Hill for the British while he returned to Boston.

VICTORY IN DEFEAT

As retreating Americans crossed Charlestown Neck, the British fired cannons at them from their ships. After the militiamen reached the mainland, they headed for their camps. They were exhausted and hungry, and some struggled under the weight of their wounded comrades. The battle on Breed's Hill, known as the Battle of Bunker Hill, was over.

American officers feared that British troops might come on the mainland to attack them at their camps at Cambridge. General Putnam ordered his Connecticut militiamen to build a protective wall at the end of Charlestown Neck. The men worked all night.

Meanwhile, on the slopes of Breed's Hill, the British worked into the night caring for 1,050 of their dead and wounded. The Americans weren't sure how many men they lost. General Ward estimated that about 450 Americans were killed, wounded, or captured.

The American revolutionary flag was flown at the Battle of Bunker Hill.

Although the Americans were forced to retreat, they showed the British that they could stand up to the greatest army in the world. There was a sort of victory in the colonists' defeat. They had fought with skill and bravery. Although the British won the battle that day, they didn't celebrate. They had lost too many soldiers, including 90 officers.

The Battle of Bunker Hill gave the British a new respect for the volunteer American militias. Now they believed the Americans might be difficult to defeat. The colonists were fighting for a cause. They wanted nothing less than a voice in decisions that affected their lives.

During the battle, Abigail Adams had watched from a few miles away. She had heard the cannons and gunfire and seen the smoke billowing from Breed's Hill. Her husband, John Adams, who would become the second president of the United States, wasn't there that day. But Abigail wrote him a letter:

Abigail Adams (1744–1818)

"The Day; perhaps the decisive Day is come on which the fate of America depends."

At that time, few Americans wanted to be fully independent of Great Britain, even after fighting the Battle of Bunker Hill. They still hoped King George would listen to their demands. But the battle damaged the colonists' already shaky relationship with Great Britain.

The Battle of Bunker Hill was the beginning of what came to be known as the Revolutionary War, or the

George III was king of England for 60 years (1760–1820), which included the American Revolution.

American War of Independence. Thousands of American soldiers would go to war for eight more years before Great Britain would give up its rule of the colonies.

A soldier in the Continental Army loaded his musket with gunpowder.

But the Battle of Bunker Hill had shown what the American army of amateur soldiers could do. These colonists could, indeed, stand up to Great Britain.

41

GLOSSARY

bayonets—blades that can be attached to the ends of rifles and used for stabbing

flank—military word for the left or right side of a battlefield; also a group of soldiers

muskets—guns with long barrels used before rifles were invented

Parliament—part of the British government that makes laws

patriots—American colonists who protested British laws and, in 1776, would support independence

provincial—local, from a particular region or colony

provisions—food, water, and weapons carried by soldiers

redoubt—a temporary defensive structure, such as a wall or ditch

reinforcements—additional military troops that bring increased strength

representation—the right of people to have a person in the legislature of a government who speaks and votes for them

42

DID YOU KNOW?

- Paul Revere is best known for his horseback ride to warn the people of Lexington and Concord that the British were coming. He was also a dentist and helped identify the body of Dr. Joseph Warren by recognizing the false teeth he had made for him before the Battle of Bunker Hill.

- Boston Harbor is deep enough for the largest ships in the world to dock there, even at low tide.

- Washington, D.C., is the only place in the United States that doesn't have elected representatives to the U.S. government. Instead of two senators and a proportionate number of representatives, Washington has one nonvoting delegate. Washington's license plates say "Taxation without Representation" so people will know that residents don't have a voting representative in Congress.

- The tea destroyed by the American patriots at the Boston Tea Party would be worth more than $3 million today.

- The average British soldier carried more than 120 pounds (54 kilograms) of equipment and supplies into battle.

IMPORTANT DATES

Timeline

1765	The Stamp Act is passed.
1767	The Townshend Duties are passed.
1768	British troops go to Boston.
1770	The Boston Massacre leaves five colonists dead.
1773	Colonists dump crates of tea into Boston Harbor at what was later called the Boston Tea Party.
1775	April 19, the battles of Lexington and Concord; April 20, the siege of Boston begins; June 17, the Battle of Bunker Hill.

IMPORTANT PEOPLE

THOMAS GAGE (1721–1787)

British general and royal governor of Massachusetts from 1773 to 1775; his mistakes at Lexington, Concord, and Bunker Hill caused him to lose his position as head of the British army in America to William Howe

WILLIAM HOWE (1729–1814)

British general who replaced Thomas Gage in October 1775 as commander in chief of the British army in America

KING GEORGE III (1738–1820)

King of England from 1760 to 1820, he eventually lost the American colonies when they declared and fought for independence

ISRAEL PUTNAM (1718–1790)

Called "Old Put" by his soldiers, he was a general for the colonial militia at Bunker Hill; when the port of Boston closed, he drove a herd of sheep to Boston from his Connecticut farm to feed Bostonians

JOSEPH WARREN (1741–1775)

A physician and American leader who volunteered to fight with the colonial militia at Bunker Hill, where he was killed in battle; his friends and enemies spoke of his friendly, fair, and honest nature

WANT TO KNOW MORE?

At the Library

Anderson, Dale. *The Causes of the American Revolution*. Milwaukee, Wis.:
World Almanac Library, 2006.

Ingram, Scott. *The Battle of Bunker Hill*. San Diego: Blackbirch
Press, 2004.

Miller, Brandon Marie. *Declaring Independence: Life During the American
Revolution*. Minneapolis: Lerner Publications Co., 2005.

Murray, Stuart. *American Revolution*. New York: DK Publishing in
association with the Smithsonian Institution, 2005.

On the Web

For more information on this topic, use FactHound.

1. Go to *www.facthound.com*

2. Type in this book ID: 075652461X

3. Click on the *Fetch It* button.

FactHound will find the best Web sites for you.

On the Road

**The Boston Historical Society
and Museum**

Old State House
206 Washington St.
Boston, MA 02109
617/720-1713
The oldest building in Boston with
paintings and artifacts from Boston's
colonial past and a crate of tea saved
from the Boston Tea Party

Bunker Hill Monument

Monument Square
Charlestown, MA 02129
617/242-5641
The site of the Battle of Bunker Hill
with a 221-foot (67-m) monument
that visitors can climb to get a great
view of Boston

Look for more We the People books about this era:

The Articles of Confederation

The Battles of Lexington and Concord

The Bill of Rights

The Boston Massacre

The Boston Tea Party

The Declaration of Independence

The Electoral College

Great Women of the American Revolution

The Minutemen

Monticello

Mount Vernon

Paul Revere's Ride

The Surrender of Cornwallis

The U.S. Constitution

Valley Forge

A complete list of We the People titles is available on our Web site:
www.compasspointbooks.com

INDEX

About the Author

Mary Englar is a freelance writer and a teacher of English and creative writing. She has a master of fine arts degree in writing from Minnesota State University and has written more than 30 nonfiction books for children. She continues to read and write about history in Minnesota.

Animales
espinosos

Animales espinosos 123

Lola M. Schaefer

Traducción de Patricia Abello

Heinemann Library
Chicago, Illinois

Customer Service 888-454-2279
Visit our website at www.heinemannlibrary.com

Designed by Sue Emerson, Heinemann Library; Page layout by Que-Net Media
Printed and bound in the United States by Lake Book Manufacturing, Inc.
Photo research by Scott Braut

08 07 06 05 04
10 9 8 7 6 5 4 3 2 1

Library of Congress Cataloging-in-Publication Data
Schaefer, Lola M., 1950-
 [Tiny-spiny animals 123. Spanish]
 Animales espinosos 123/ Lola M. Schaefer; traducción de Patricia Abello.
       p. cm. -- (Animales espinosos)
Summary: Spiny animals introduce the numbers from one to ten.
  ISBN 1-4034-4303-3 (HC) -- ISBN 1-4034-4309-2 (Pbk.)
  1. Counting--Juvenile literature. 2. Spines (Zoology)--Juvenile literature. [1. Armored animals. 2. Counting. 3. Spanish language materials.] I. Title: Animales espinosos uno, dos, tres. II. Title.
  QA113.S382518 2003
  513.2'11--dc21

                                              2003049941

Acknowledgments
The author and publishers are grateful to the following for permission to reproduce copyright material:
p. 3 Gerald & Buff Corsi/Visuals Unlimited; p. 5 E & P Bauer/Bruce Coleman Inc.; p. 7 Alan Blank/Bruce Coleman Inc.; p. 9 Raymond A. Mendez/Animals Animals; p. 11 Kjell B. Sandved/Visuals Unlimited; p. 13 The Pelican Lagoon Research Centre; p. 15 D. P. Wilson/FLPA; p. 17 Anthony Bannister/Gallo Images/Corbis; p. 19 Brandon D. Cole/Corbis; p. 21 Andrew J. Martinez/Photo Researchers, Inc.; p. 22 T. Kitchin and V. Hurst/NHPA; p. 23 (column 1, T-B) Leonard Lee Rue III/Animals Animals, Corbis, Jeff Rotman/Photo Researchers, Inc.; (column 2, T-B) P. Parks/OSF/Animals Animals, Anthony Bannister/Gallo Images/Corbis, Brandon D. Cole/Corbis; p. 24 David Welling/Animals Animals; back cover (L-R) Raymond A. Mendez/Animals Animals, Mitsuaki Iwago/Minden Pictures

Cover photographs by (L-R) Gary Meszaros/Bruce Coleman Inc., E & P Bauer/Bruce Coleman Inc., Scott W. Smith/Animals Animals

Every effort has been made to contact copyright holders of any material reproduced in this book. Any omissions will be rectified in subsequent printings if notice is given to the publisher.

Special thanks to our advisory panel for their help in the preparation of this book:

Anita R. Constantino
Literacy Specialist
Irving Independent School District
Irving, TX

Leah Radinsky
Bilingual Teacher
Inter-American Magnet School
Chicago, IL

Aurora Colón García
Reading Specialist
Northside Independent School District
San Antonio, TX

Ursula Sexton
Researcher, WestEd
San Ramon, CA

Unas palabras están en negrita, **así.**
Las encontrarás en el glosario en fotos de la página 23.

Uno   1

Un equidna excava la tierra en busca de comida.

Dos   2

Dos puerco espines están sentados en un árbol.

Usan sus **garras** para treparse.

Tres   3

Un lagarto cornudo hembra puso tres huevos.

¡De los huevos saldrán tres **crías!**

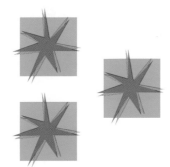

Cuatro 4

Los puerco espines
tienen cuatro dientes
anaranjados.

Son grandes y afilados.

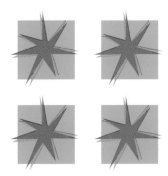

Cinco 5

La boca de los erizos
de mar tiene cinco
dientes.

Usan los dientes
para comer.

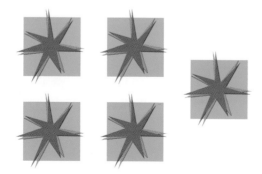

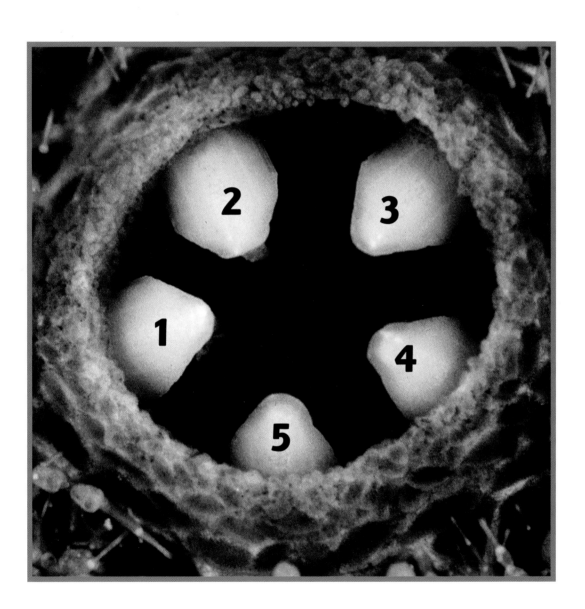

Seis 6

Aquí hay seis equidnas pequeñitos.

Algunos equidnas pueden vivir en el **bosque.**

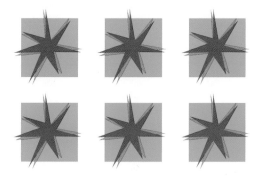

Siete   7

Aquí hay siete huevos
de erizos de mar.

De los huevos saldrán
sus crías, llamadas **larvas**.

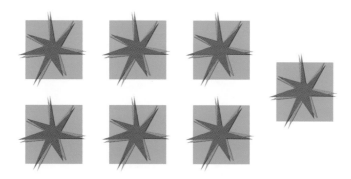

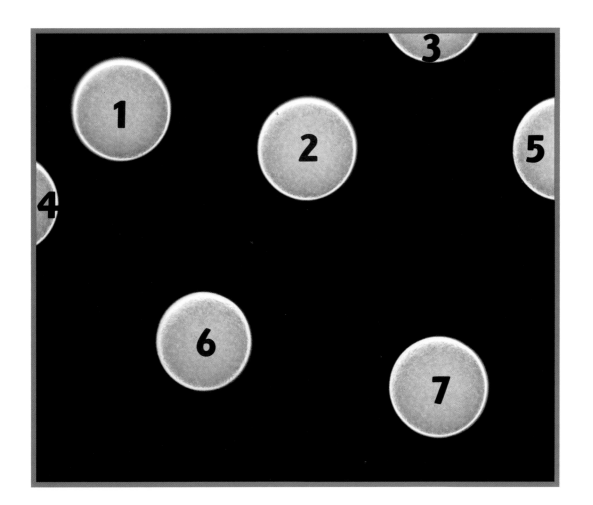

Ocho 8

Aquí hay ocho **melones.**

Algunos puerco espines comen melones.

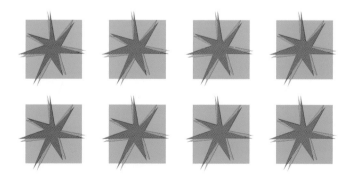

Nueve　9

La concha de los erizos
de mar se llama **testa.**

Aquí hay nueve testas.

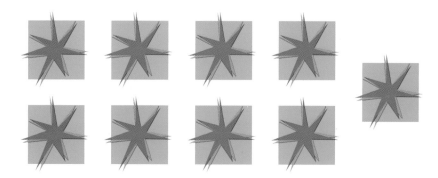

Diez   10

Aquí hay diez erizos
de mar.

Comen unas algas
marinas llamadas **kelp.**

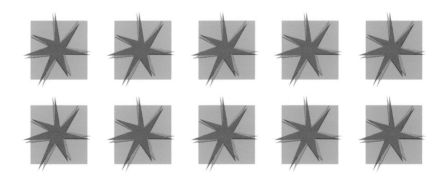

¡Míralo bien!

¿Cuántos puerco espines están sentados en este tronco?

Busca la respuesta en la página 24.